Tru–An American Princess

A Fairy Tale Every Girl Should Read

Includes 12 Life Applications

Linda Trimble

**STRONG
PUBLISHING
House**

Bringing the strength of your words to reality

Tru—An American Princess
A Fairy Tale Every Girl Should Read
Linda Trimble

Published by: Strong Publishing House
www.strongpublishinghouse.com
For publishing inquiries contact:
Lawrence Trimble, CEO
strongpublishinghouse@gmail.com

Dedication

This book is dedicated to my lovely daughters
that my husband and I had the privilege of parenting—
the three princesses. Today, we are grateful to God for
their lives and their ability to walk in their purpose. God
birthed them through their biological parents, but allowed
us to experience parenthood as the King and Queen of our
home. They are truly special women today. I dedicate this
book to our first and only granddaughter (at the time of this
writing) who has known she was a princess since she
entered this world. She is gifted and bright with a heart of
gold. When she was 2 years old a lady in the grocery store
told her how beautiful she was. The lady said, "You are
just a little princess," my granddaughter's response was "I
know it!" I first thought she was being rude, and asked her
"why didn't you say thank you?" to which she replied,
"grandmother you always tell me that I am a princess so I
was just telling her that I know it because you already told
me that I was." That was classic! We know the desire of
all parents is for their children to grow up knowing their
own identity and loving themselves. This book is also
dedicated to my other daughters who lived with me at one
time or another, and those who stayed for short or long
periods of time just to receive what God had for them in
order to walk in their purpose. Finally, I dedicate this book
to all of my spiritual sons and daughters past, present, and
future. Thank you for being faithful.

Thank you to my publisher who was just as dedicated to this project as I was. He saw the vision and helped me to bring it out. He is so gifted and anointed, and is also the first son that God gave us.

Thanks to my co-worker who is always encouraging and inspiring me to fulfill the call of God, and promising that she will be with me.

Thank you to my family, my five wonderful brothers who always pushed me to the limit in everything, my nieces and adopted nieces who are all in my girls-circle. To my sister who has always believed in me and who always wants only what was best for me. I am grateful for my loving parents who I treasure and I am grateful for having had them as parents.

To the man in my life, my husband, who knows just what to say to me and always at the right time. He said "The qualities of a true princess sound just like you." Lord, I love that man! To the other men in my life, my grandsons, they are priceless!

Most of all, my Heavenly Father is to be glorified. I give honor to Him for everything! Without Him I am nothing and can do nothing, but through Him I can do all that He calls me to do. He changed my entire life. He has brought me out of so much, and was with me through everything. I am who I am today because I can see through His eyes now. Amen!

<u>Foreword</u>

Why this book?

This book is about purpose and destiny. It is about living your dreams. It is about being happy and fulfilled in life. It is about finding yourself. It is about understanding deception; but more importantly, it is about understanding your identity. This fairy tale will surely help each reader (child and adult) find out why he or she was born and for what purpose.

A fairy tale is normally a children's story about magical and imaginary beings and lands. The Merriam Webster dictionary says that it is a false story about magical creatures that is meant to trick people. This fairy tale is about a false story that will bring truth and revelation to you, especially those who may be bound in poverty and want. If you have experienced hurt, shame, abuse, or any type of rejection in life, then this fairy tale is for you. This fairy tale is not like any other: Instead of tricking you, it will uncover the greatest deception that is in the world today.

No more will you have to dream of being a princess, prince, queen or king, because this fairy tale will disclose how you are already connected to royalty. You can start living the life of royalty using the truths revealed in this fairy tale.

You are an heir of royalty and all its rights and privileges. You might be saying, how? Well, you have to read the book, but you will find your answer.

The King is summoning you!

Honorable Linda Trimble
Of the Royal Priesthood
Holy Nation Family of God

Contents

Qualities of A Princess

An American Princess is characterized by her qualities.
Tru definitely shares the qualities of a princess. A princess
of any nation, culture or family is characterized by these
qualities. A princess is a noble young lady who carries
herself with poise and dignity. She listens attentively. And
when she speaks, she carefully chooses her words. She
exercises control over her emotions and makes choices
based on what's right rather than on how she feels. Though
she isn't perfect, she possesses a strong sense of duty that
comes with knowing she's a princess. A princess thinks of
others. She is trusting and faithful. Another princess virtue
is humility. She doesn't demand or expect special
treatment from others and chooses to refrain from bragging
or boasting. Instead, she focuses on others and their needs.
She doesn't have to be in the spotlight because she already
knows she's a princess. A princess is extraordinarily
beneficent. She is gentle, generous, compassionate, patient,
good-natured and forgiving. A princess doesn't compete
with her prince. She does just the opposite, she builds him
up. It's her admiration and respect that inspire the prince
and compel him to greatness. A princess is a princess
regardless of her attire or her circumstances.

There is a princess in every girl; filled with the desire to be beautiful, to be lavished with gifts and niceties, and especially to be able to wear a crown. Little do we believe that we are quite the princesses already, and the inheritance is already ours. This book is about Tru, an American girl who happens to be a princess; but it is also about any girl, woman, or person who ever had a dream or vision of being a prince or princess.

"People become really quite remarkable when they start thinking that they can do things. When they believe in themselves, they have the first secret of success. Successful people respond rather than react to negative situations. They tend to be independent of others opinion, and respond to situations in a manner which will produce the best outcome, as opposed to what is best for their ego."

~Norman Vincent Peale

Prologue
Tru–An American Princess

Main characters: The Evil Genius, Triston; the American girl, Tru; the designer and toaster, Amari; the Great King; a husband and wife with five children; a family with a business and a car; a bank and a banker; a Toaster Business with a toaster and burned toast; a violent gang banger; a drug addict, a bank robber; a group of children singing and dancing; a trumpet player to sound the trumpet; and men to carry the princess' bed to the king. The characters are fictional; however, they resemble the lives of people we all know and love.

Setting: A town with a lemonade stand, a family, a school, a bed, a church, a business, a husband, and a wife. Families also have a peach cobbler, a baseball game, a car and a place where Tru can go and pray. The town also consists of homes, clothes, toys, apple pies, townspeople and children. There is one family with its own business and car. The husband and wife have five children. Triston has lots of money, clothes and material things. Tru holds her treasure of a pretty teapot, chamomile tea, and a garden of fruit and berries very dear to her heart.

Tru, a beautiful girl: Tru (pronounced Troo) is a strikingly beautiful bronze-colored maiden with dark colored eyes and soft curls in her hair. She resembles a fawn just out of the brush with awestruck eyes looking for her mom. Tru is a dreamer. Whatever she dreams will come true. She is so loving and kind that she can only dream of good things for others. She believes that if she dreams for herself, her dreams would be selfish acts that she would not dare to do on purpose. Many know that Tru has the gift of dreams and will often try to influence her dreams for their own selfish gain. People, therefore, always surround her.

Introduction

This story is about an American girl whose name is Tru. Tru is being held captive by the deception of an evil genius. She believes she is just a common girl and has no true identity. The acts of the evil genius are more than she can bear sometimes. He has a way of providing the people with just enough to get along; however, no one really knows that they can have more. Tru, the American girl, must find her true identity and abilities for herself. The journey starts in Tru's own soul, where she begins her search for more because, deep inside, she knows there has to be more to life than what she has. Tru has heard about a country where a Great King lives. Her heart's desire is to one day meet the Great King and discover the secret of true greatness. Though she lives under the great deception of believing that she cannot have anything for herself, she is a dreamer and dreams wonderful dreams for others. The ability to have these types of dreams makes her really special and unique. Most people are selfish and only want to dream or wish for things for themselves–but no, not Tru! She would not dare dream for herself or dream negative things about anyone else. She is much too noble in her heart.

Life Application #1

The Spirit of Deception

Someone who is deceived "has accepted as true or valid what is false or invalid" (Webster). Likewise, the one who deceives others convinces them to accept, as truth, something false. Paul, in the Book of I Timothy (2:14), references one of the best Biblical examples of deception, saying: "And Adam was not deceived, but the woman being deceived, fell into transgression." Eve knew the truth, but the serpent convinced her that God had told her a lie. There are covenant promises that cannot be broken, made out to us in the great Book of Wisdom called the Bible. The Great King said that all nations would be blessed through a certain person's seed. We are entitled to every promise He has made, and the only way we do not inherit the promised blessings is if we are deceived to believe that they do not exist for us. There has been a very diabolic scheme unleashed to destroy that certain seed since that time. Although woman messed up, fell for the lies and became prey to the tricks and schemes of the evil one, the Great King already had an alternate plan that was better than the first one. He made a way for us to inherit our blessings and to become aware of the snares and tactics of any type of deception or trickery. He gave us a spirit of Love and Power, along with a Sound mind, to overcome the fear and timidity of the threat and operation of the spirit of deception.

The spirit of deception is one of the major causes of the loss of true identity and the captivity of the people. Freedom only comes when the true self is recognized and accepted. You can be a pauper, prince or a king and not know your true identity. If you do not know who you are, you will experience bondage and captivity. Uncovering who you are and your origin will reveal not only your true self, but also the power and gifts that lie within. Purposes are established when untapped potential is realized. When you come from royalty, but live like an indigent, then you will live beneath your blessings and purpose. As part of a royal family and holy nation, we should live in peace and contentment. Anyone can be deceived; nevertheless, there is a way to recognize deception and to live above the traps that are planned for you. The evil genius distorts your view of yourself and cheats you out of a blessed life of abundance and plenty. The evil genius will cloud your view so that you will not be able to see the great things in store for your life. You have to look within your heart and soul and be in constant pursuit of your destiny and purpose while looking to the Great King. As children of royalty, we can live free from bondage, and as members of the Royal Priesthood and Holy Nation family of the Great King, we can fulfill our destiny and purpose. The story uncovers the acts and operations of the evil genius in our society. He is the one who wishes to keep us down by giving us just enough and who keeps us acting in selfish and sometimes violent ways.

Chapter 1

The Noble City of Tyrina

Tru lived in a city called Tyrina (pronounced Ti-re-na), which is considered the land of the noble. The city is located in the heart of the Great Country of Lambert. Tru knew that Lambert was the land where all the great people lived. However, the citizens of Tyrina were taught that the great people were those who lived inside the walls of the city. The evil genius wanted the people of the city to believe that they were the only great people and that they should only measure themselves by themselves. The noble people in the city of Tyrina believed that they were great (but only in their own eyes). They believed that great people had one great car that everyone took turns driving. They had one great building that everyone used for business. They had one great school where all children attended. They had one great temple where everyone attended for worship. The sad thing was that they rarely went into the temple for worship or for anything else. They did not attend frequently enough to know that within the great temple was the key to true greatness. In the Great Temple of Worship the people of Tyrina will make some great discoveries later.

Tru, an authentic noble person, lived with her noble family in Tyrina, the land of the noble. Tyrina was the only city that was supposed to have truly noble citizens. Noble families lived in Tyrina and conducted themselves in very noble ways. They married other nobles, had noble children, built noble homes, and attended the noble school. The noble fathers worked at noble jobs. The noble mothers baked the best peach cobblers and apple pies, and made the most flavorful lemonade in all the land. The favorite pastime for all the noble people was to watch a noble baseball game.

Chapter 2

Tru Possessed the Gift of Dreams

Now, Tru (who had the gift of dreams) would dream often. She dreamt especially after having been in the presence of someone who could imagine the future or life in the Great City in the great country of Lambert. One day Tru's dreams were like none that she had ever dreamed before. Tru dreamt that in the Great City there lived a Great King, who could do great things, exceedingly, abundantly and above all that anyone could ask or think. Because Tru was from Tyrina, the land of the noble, she would not dare ask for anything for herself in her dreams. Therefore, she kept this dream hidden in her heart and hoped it would go away. However, she kept dreaming the same thing over and over. As a noble person, she believed that it would be completely selfish to wish her own dream would come true for herself. After all, Tru was taught that to be noble was for everyone to have the same thing and only have enough, not more than enough.

If she dreamed of having more than others had or of having an abundance of things, it would mean that she was not humble and noble.

Chapter 3

Triston, the Evil Genius

Triston, the evil genius, also lived in the land of the noble, the city of Tyrina. He did noble acts, but he wasn't noble in his heart. He knew Tru had the gift of dreams, so he was jealous and envious of her. He had more evil in his heart than good. When he would go into town and see people talking to Tru, he would become enraged because he knew that their conversations would influence her dreams.

Chapter 4

Society in the Noble City of Tyrina

Everybody would ride in the one great car to go shopping for groceries, clothes, and toys. Each person would get a little something and be satisfied (or at least it appeared as if they were satisfied). As soon as someone ran out of groceries, he or she would borrow from the next person, then he or she would have to borrow from the next. Clothes would not last long because the children would grow so fast. The little ones were all right because they could wear the hand-me-downs from the others. However, the teenagers and young adults wanted more and did not truly understand noble ways and humble means. Toys were not as big a deal because the small children had one each that they could collect and keep from year to year unless a toy was broken. No one was supposed to act selfishly in the great city of Tyrina because the people were to be noble and always do what was noble and right. At the beginning, violence was almost non-existent in the noble city. The people were right in their own eyes, and no one could tell them differently. People in Tyrina only compared themselves to themselves inside their own city walls. They were told this is how everyone lived, even in the Great City.

When Tru finished visiting with the townspeople and after genuinely caring for their problems and families, their personal problems and issues now influenced her dreams. She would go home, retire for the evening, fall asleep and dream. Once she dreamt that one noble family had a car and a business of its own. The dream came true for that one noble family. Another time she dreamt that a certain man and his wife, who previously could not have children, had five. The dream came true for this certain man and his wife who could not have children.

If one of the families in the city of Tyrina progressed more than another family, the progressive family would help another family to progress. They would relish in their achievements, which would add to their future successes as well as their neighboring families. One success depends on another; but there were evil spirits lurking, and the families were not aware of the actions of the evil spirits. The spirits were let loose in the town through the evil genius, who would eventually not allow this type of prosperity to continue. One tactic used was to try to get the townspeople not to help each other and only use their resources for themselves to get ahead. Noble people live by the secret principle that one is a success only if the entire town is a success. Genuine care is to genuinely care about others. Tru understood that, deep within, the secret to her success was to help others, and that was what she was all about. Tru was noble in her heart.

Life Application #2

True Success

    When you were born, your purpose was already established. Your abilities, gifts, and talents are already inside. They are a part of your genetic makeup. You could spend a lifetime trying to figure them out if you do not consult with the One who designed each part before you were born. Some gifts are more prominent than others, which sometimes causes people to want to possess what they do not have. This means one may be envious of someone else's gift. If your gift is more prominent or clearly seen and used more openly, it can be easily mistaken for the best gift of all. The other person looking on may envy your gift and not cultivate his or her own gift. Sometimes people get envious of the popularity of another person when that person may simply have a more outgoing personality or is more of an extrovert than an introvert. Popularity should not be used to define a person's worth. No one should ever need to measure another's worth. You measure your own worth by asking yourself, "Have I done the best that I could with what God gave me?" Your gifts and talents are used as a service to mankind. If you are here on this earth right now, you have a gift, a purpose, and some form of service to offer while you are here in this world. That specific gift, purpose, or service is what your life should be about. Your gift will cause you to be in good health, good financial status, and good standing with God and man. Divine favor is in your life's purpose, which means you have the grace to do it.

The city of Tyrina was considered a great city by those who lived there, because the people were noble. However, to be truly noble, you have to first believe in yourself. You have to know what you have inside and trust your own abilities. One of the major keys is that you not only know what you possess inside, but you also use it for the good of others. The people in the city of Tyrina had jobs, homes, schools, etc., and seemed to be alright—but they were deceived into thinking that they had everything they were supposed to have. The number one problem was that they failed to go into the great temple for worship. In the great temple is the key to true greatness. See, "in the Middle Ages, there was a definite structure in society. You were born into a class of people and generally stayed in that class for your entire life. Working hard did not change your status. Your clothing, food, marriage, homes, etc., were determined for you. After the rank of king, the hierarchy was the nobles, the knights, the clergy (religious people), the tradesmen and the peasants" (Western Reserve Public Media). In keeping with this lifestyle, you can see why the people were so comfortable. In the Middle Ages, the culture of nobles was classed or ranked right under the King, but there was a lot of control. In this day and time, in our position as believers, we are ranked right under the Great King. We should not be comfortable until we understand our relationship and our dominion, and have tapped into all that we have access to in our kingdom. The great temple supplied the people with the knowledge they needed, but they would not go in to find out. Let's not act that same way and fail to go into the temple to find out about the key to true greatness, or to identify with the Great King of all kings. The people of Tyrina were apparently ignorant of their rights and privileges and operated as nobles in some ways, but were very limited in other ways. From their perspective they were good because they only compare themselves with themselves. They did not have more than enough and barely had enough, and they never had enough for others. It is obvious that there is something evil lurking to take away our ability to think and produce wealth and resources for ourselves. There seems to be a well thought out plan to keep nations of people in lack and poverty.

According to www.businessdictionary.com, poverty is a condition in which people's basic needs for food, clothing, and shelter are not being met. Poverty is generally one of two types: Absolute poverty or relative poverty. Absolute poverty is synonymous with destitution and occurs when people cannot obtain adequate resources (measured in terms of calories or nutrition) to support a minimum level of physical health. Absolute poverty means about the same everywhere, and can be eradicated as demonstrated by some countries. Relative poverty occurs when people do not enjoy a certain minimum level of living standards as determined by a government (and enjoyed by the bulk of the population) that vary from country to country, sometimes within the same country. Relative poverty occurs everywhere, is said to be increasing, and may never be eradicated.

People define success in different ways. Success can be defined as the accomplishment of an aim or purpose. Most people want to know the end results before they start a thing. Poverty is just a condition, but success is so much more than your condition. You may have a condition today, but tomorrow you could have success. Your life is already designed for you to succeed. Some people think it is only the attainment of popularity or profit. Success is not true success until you are in purpose. Read below a few quotes about success spoken by some very wise, spiritual, and successful people. This kind of wisdom will help you fulfill purpose.

Ralph Waldo Emerson on Success:
To laugh often and much.
To win the respect of intelligent people and the affection of children.
To earn the appreciation of honest critics and endure the betrayal of false friends.
To appreciate beauty; to find the best in others.
To leave the world a bit better.

Walt Disney on Success:
Think tomorrow – make today's effort pay off tomorrow.
Free the imagination – you are capable of more than you can imagine—so imagine the ultimate.
Have fun while achieving goals—you are never truly a success until you enjoy what you are doing.

Anglican Bishop (from around 1100 AD) on Success

When I was young and free my imagination had no limits, I dreamed of changing the world. As I grew older and wiser, I discovered that the world would not change, so I decided to change my country. It too, seemed unmovable.

As I grew into my twilight years, in one last desperate attempt, I settled for changing my family and those closest to me. They would have none of it. And now as I lay on my deathbed, I suddenly realize, if I had only changed myself first, then by example I would have changed my family. From their inspiration and encouragement, I would have been able to better my community, city, country, and who knows—I may have even changed the world.

Bishop T.D. Jakes on Success

Even successful people have self-doubt, but they don't succumb to it. Everybody has some angst, some fear, some negative voice saying, 'Who are you?' But some people rebuke it and other people birth it. The difference between rebuking it and birthing it is how long you nurture the thought.

Jeremiah 29:11 on Success

For I know the plans I have for you, declares the Lord, plans to prosper you and not to harm you, plans to give you hope and a future.

Webster

Success is the favorable or prosperous termination of attempts or endeavors; the accomplishment of one's goals.

Norman Vincent Peale on Success

Formulate and stamp indelibly on your mind a mental picture of yourself as succeeding. Hold this picture tenaciously. Never permit it to fade. Your mind will seek to develop the picture. . .Do not build up obstacles in your imagination.

Jerry Bruckner on Success

Success is not a destination; it is a continuous journey of striving toward your important goals that never ends.

Norman Vincent Peale on Success

People become really quite remarkable when they start thinking that they can do things. When they believe in themselves, they have the first secret of success.
Successful people respond rather than react to negative situations. They tend to be independent of others opinion, and respond to situations in a manner which will produce the best outcome, as opposed to what is best for their ego.

Eleanor Roosevelt on Success

No one can make you feel inferior without your consent.

Linda Trimble on Success

Success is the fulfillment of your purpose to turn out as God has planned.

Chapter 5

Characteristics of the Evil Genius

The evil genius, Triston, was always able to influence people to give him what he wanted. His influence caused him to have so much in the form of money, clothes, land, and things that he did not know what to do with half of the things he possessed. The one thing he did not have was Tru's ability to dream. He wanted to have the ability to dream so that he could always have people come to talk to him. He thought if he could dream like Tru and his dreams came true, he would have everything he wanted—including the rulership of Tyrina and the rest of the Great Country of Lambert. Triston had so much evil in his heart that he thought evil all the time. Since the beginning of his captivity, he was only able to see the negative sides of people and life. Triston did not even know he was a captive. He thought he knew everything and had control of others. He was basically a tyrant and used manipulation, aggression, control, and evil to get his way with the citizens of Tyrina. He was so deceived that he did not realize he was also in captivity.

Life Application #3

The Origin of Evil

    Paul told Timothy (1 Tim. 6:10) that the "Love of Money is the root of all evil." A better rendering of this verse is in the New International Version of the Bible, "For the love of money is a root of all kinds of evil. Some people, eager for money, have wandered from the faith and pierced themselves with many griefs." There are people in this world today who have evil ways and actions and are in darkness to the true source of goodness and life. Greed for money, power, and position or popularity is surely a key to all kinds of evil thoughts and deeds. If a person's mind is in captivity by these, he or she cannot see much good in others. The people whose minds have been set free from captivity have to be diligent in hurling away every evil thought that enters the mind. Casting evil thoughts down is difficult for those whose minds are in captivity because it is hard to separate the evil ways and actions from their own evil thoughts. They are so used to acting on their own thoughts and impulses instead of in the freedom that comes from love and truth, until the ability to distinguish an evil thought from a good and wholesome thought is very limited. Most of these types of individuals, like Triston, have been held captive through some evil genius practice and live under dark deception. Triston's greed for popularity with the people was really about control or power over others. If he acquired the power, then he would have the money.

No one seems to really know when evil began on Earth. In Genesis there is an account that describes Earth as being without form and void. This description depicts chaos and evil. There is a reference to a distinction between two trees in the garden: first, The Tree of the Knowledge of Good and Evil; and second, the Tree of Life. Both trees were forbidden at different times. One tree was forbidden immediately when man was given his dominion and assignment in the garden. The other tree was forbidden after the man committed the act of disobedience. Man not only disrespected the garden he was protecting, but also the owner of the garden. The reference to the woman being deceived was pretty significant in the book of 1 Timothy; however, the male had something else going on. Both the man and the woman could have stopped the course of evil in this world, but they did not. Since the man was not deceived, he should have made a wise decision and ordered the evil out of the garden, but he did not. This act of disobedience would cause the rest of us to contend with the test of disobedience. This deception causes mankind to get trapped in a state of captivity by evil thoughts and desires. The Great King had to banish man and woman from the garden to save them from themselves. What may have seemed evil or harsh was actually a divine act of the Great King saving man and woman from destruction. Because of the sin in this world today, the Great King is still giving us the opportunity to resist partaking of The Tree of the Knowledge of Good and Evil, and the Tree of Life in a fallen condition. He is saying to us to rise up and realize who we are and live like we are of the Royal Kingdom now, and one day we will partake of the Tree of Life and live forever.

To be insecure is characteristic of a person being influenced by evil. It is easy to seek approval from those around you or become resentful of the gifts and callings of others. Some people are very unappreciative of their own gifts and callings because they continue to compare themselves to others. If you lost your identity early in life, you must seek your own identity now. If you have feelings of anxiety, distrust, and fear, or you are unkind to others and cannot support the gifts and callings of others, I urge you to seek to know your true self more and more. The evil genius represents that negative boyfriend or friend who suggests that you are not worth it. He represents that person who cannot celebrate you, but who continues to point out your flaws and imperfections. The evil genius will even manipulate your thoughts into thinking something is wrong with your greatest qualities and attributes. However, when you know the true secret of success in your life, nothing can bring you down.

Life Application #4

Characteristics, Traits, and Labels to Avoid

   Our nation is experiencing an identity crisis. People are separated by ethnic origin, race, and color of skin. Those characteristics alone should not define you or your rights and privileges of the Royal Priesthood, Holy Nation Family of the Great King. Once you discover your kingdom connection, you become aware of your new nature and real identity. You begin to realize you are of the royal kingdom and there is no identity crisis, no division, no prejudice, no superiority, and no lowly, disdained members; but all are equally blessed, enriched, and enthralled by the honor of our Great King.

   The evil influences in the world can affect us only if we allow them to affect us. These influences from the world are all orchestrated by the evil genius. They appear as fun, games and harmless acts; but in actuality, they are smart and cunningly devised tricks and schemes to distort your dreams and future. For example, alcohol is a strong beverage that people drink socially and supposedly responsibly; however, alcohol is the most commonly used addictive substance in the U.S. In fact, 17.6 million people, or one in every 12 adults, suffer from alcohol abuse or dependence, along with several million more who engage in risky drinking patterns that could lead to alcohol problems. Addiction is a primary complex brain disorder that can alter your way of life. Our streets are poisoned with it along with drugs, violence, and all manner of crime.

Some 33,000 violent street gangs, motorcycle gangs, and prison gangs with about 1.4 million members are criminally active in the U.S. today. Many are sophisticated and well organized; all use violence to control neighborhoods and boost their illegal moneymaking activities, which include robbery, drug and gun trafficking, fraud, extortion, and prostitution rings. According to the 2011 National Gang Threat Assessment report, gangs are responsible for an average of 48 percent of violent crime in most jurisdictions, and up to 90 percent in others (per Fbi.gov/statistics).

A gangbanger simply is that person who exposes his weaknesses by exploiting other people. The gangbanger ultimately is labeled as a participant in the promotion of violence, illicit sex, and sometimes distribution of illegal drugs; and has been associated with several important risk factors. These risk factors are variables that increase the likelihood of the outcome in question—in this case, gang membership. Gang research scholars have identified the following risk factors:

- *Learning disabilities & emotional disorders (60% to 78% of incarcerated gang members—male and female—have emotional and learning disabilities)*
- *School failure and truancy*
- *No involvement in positive activities outside of school*
- *Friends and peers who are delinquent*
- *Early involvement in petty theft and behavioral disorders in grade school*
- *Low income*

[Source: Google.com/ganginvolvement]

Risk factors are unmet needs and cause those most affected to react in dark and evil ways. This area of understanding gang banging, prostitution, and drug addiction is a very good look into the darkness of this world. These can be classified as behaviors produced due to the factors of poverty and want.

The most commonly used and most abused drug is marijuana. Other common drugs of abuse include cocaine, heroin, inhalants, and prescription drugs, including pain relievers, depressants and stimulants. Even if a person is prescribed a medication, taking more of that drug than the recommended dosage is dangerous.

Sexual immorality includes prostitution, unchastity, fornication and every kind of unlawful sexual intercourse, as well as any kind of illegitimate sexual intercourse. This also includes any extra-marital intercourse or illicit physical sexual intercourse with someone who is not the person's God-approved spouse. [Source: Apologetic Press.org]

Identity is being who or what a person or thing was created to be. If you are created in royalty, then be royalty. If you are created in greatness, then be great. If you are created in love, then be love. If you are created in prosperity, then be prosperous. If you know your creator, you will understand your identity. If you were created in the image of God, then be godly. You cannot truly identify with evil and destruction. Evil may have become a part of you who are reading this book, but it is not you. You were born into royalty. It is a kingdom that is not anything like this present world. If the enemy has deceived you, it is now up to you to latch on to the truth and apply every strategy in this book to change your future back to what was intended. You were not born to be a gangster, prostitute, or a drug addict. These are the results of certain behaviors (character traits and labels). You were born to be great in the Kingdom.

Chapter 6

Unselfish and Wholesome Dreams

Tru's dreams were unselfish and wholesome. She could see life in so many different ways. People loved her dreams because her picturesque visions were filled with good things, encouragement, and purpose. She was filled with plans, expectations, and life. Tru made others happy, but could not see through the evil deception that was cast upon her. She longed to dream for herself; however, her noble heart caused her dreams to be unselfish and only for the people.

Life Application #5

Fulfill the Dreams of Your Heart

God can divinely give dreams to you! Let's talk about the dream where you see yourself doing great things or things you like doing. You wake up in the morning thinking about these things. When you go to bed at night, you are thinking about either doing them or how to do them. Just the thought of these things makes you want to get up and start your day.

Dreams are more than just a succession of images, thoughts, or emotions passing through the mind during sleep. [Source: dictionary.reference.com] Dreams are the visions of your future. Dreams are the things (plans and purposes) that play out in your head when you are being inspired by the power of the gifts and special talents you have been endowed with on the inside. These dreams are the driving forces to your future. From childhood, these dreams begin to unfold; and as you grow and learn, these dreams should develop more and more. Parents, teachers, community, and religious leaders are all a part of this development process because it is so important for every single person to grow and learn in order for his or her dreams to come true. How can you not fulfill the dreams of your heart? It can easily happen because if the process of learning and growing is inhibited, then dreams can be thwarted. Disillusionment happens and people stop dreaming because they are discouraged. If we live in lands like Tyrina, Tru's hometown, where people never venture outside of their own walls, your dreams will be very limited. When dreams are limited, you stop believing that you can achieve them. Your dreams are almost always bigger than your present situation and they can seem impossible to achieve. However, dreams are the part of you that helps you to achieve things in life. Go after your dreams! Follow the process—parents train you, teachers impart more knowledge to you, community members inspire you, and your religious leaders ignite you.

How can you fulfill your dreams?

1. *Start with examining your dreams— determine which are God-given and divine. What is it that you think of the most? What do you think about doing that you are not already doing now? If it is divine, it will be something that will benefit others and bring blessings back to you as well.*

2. *Parenting the dream is the duty of parents.*
   Children are a heritage of the Lord! It is important
   that parents bring them up right—in the nurture and
   admonition of the Lord. Parents must train and
   children must learn from parents the simple things
   in life such as respect, obedience to authority,
   patience, kindness, etc. These trainings will help
   anyone go a long way in life. When a child is a
   child, everything is a learning opportunity: Family
   time, play time, family devotion, family vacation,
   etc. Children are a part of every aspect of family
   life. The children may not pay the bills in the
   house, but they should learn by how you pay the
   bills. Children may not go to work or own the
   business, but they should learn by how you go to
   work or run your business. Parents cultivate your
   dreams to help you stay focused in life and not lose
   your way. Some parents are over-protective or
   strict with rules and guidelines; however, they are
   cultivating your dreams. If you have very strict
   parents, it is because the Great King planned it that
   way because He knew you needed it. Over-
   protective and strict does not mean abusive

parenting. If there is abuse in your household (such as beatings, name calling, degrading remarks, withholding of food or clothes, sexual advances, etc.), please talk to a counselor, clergy, or social worker. There is deception lurking everywhere. Parents are sometimes deceived, too.

3. *Teachers are a major factor in the lives of children. When a teacher imparts knowledge in such a way that it causes the children to learn more than the teacher can ever teach them, that's an inspiring teacher. Teachers teach. but they should also inspire children to learn. When you learn something or acquire new knowledge, doesn't it make you feel something? Does it make you want to share your newly acquired knowledge with others? Your inspiration to share with others is how you can determine if a teacher is really teaching you something. All teachers may not be as inspiring as you would like them to be, but learn all you can from them anyway. You will be able to use it again at some point in life.*

4. *Community is the village raising the child. There should not be one community in this world that is not willing to invest in its children. If this nation really wanted to make the world a better place, then it should invest in the children. Better schools, better neighborhood housing, top of the line community centers, after-school programs, and quality playgrounds would give our children a greater chance of survival more than you think. Children do not need to raise themselves. Everyone has a responsibility to contribute to the well-being of others, especially the children. The contribution you make to your community is another effort to inspire a child or children.*

5. *Religious leaders in your life should be the matches that ignite the fire. If a preacher, prophet, or a king could help a child or person get in touch with his or her creator, his job is almost done. Everything comes with instructions from its creator or originator. The person or thing created is better off with the original instruction manual. A religious leader should be skillfully equipped with the proper instructions to help you find and fulfill your*

purpose. One of the greatest leaders of Israel was instructed very wisely on how to turn out as the creator had planned. He was instructed as such: "This Book of the Law shall not depart from your mouth, but you shall meditate on it day and night, so that you may be careful to do according to all that is written in it. For then you will make your way prosperous, and then you will have good success" (Joshua 1:8 New Standard Version)

Life Application #6

Achieving Your Dreams

    Stop and think about what is affecting your dreams and future. Evil influence is all around to distract you from your purpose and destiny. Anything can distort your focus, especially if you do not know your own value and worth. The trick is in the destruction of one's true identity. Destruction and violence are all around, and unless true identity is recognized, true greatness is not achieved. As evil prevails, the enemy's sole purpose is to inhibit the knowledge and understanding of a person's identity.

    What is affecting your dreams and future? Do you really know who you are? Are you just an offspring of your parents? Do you know that you were born of a royal seed according to your bloodline? What if your mom or dad were descendants of a King such as King David of Judah? King David was multi-gifted and talented. He was a true warrior, writer, and musician. He rose to power and greatness after serving in obscurity simply because of his bloodline. He served another king, King Saul of Benjamin. Because King David was anointed king as a young teen, he had to maintain his focus and kingly lineage. He had a plan that he did not allow to fail. There was nothing that could be done to keep David from being anointed as King, because he was born for it. All people on this earth belong to royalty. We are all descendants of Adam, which makes David your cousin. One of Adam's grandsons, Abraham, had a son called Isaac, and Isaac's son was called Jacob. Jacob was the father of 12 sons, but the one called Judah carried the special seed that would bring forth the child that would connect us all back to the royal family of David. Jesus Christ was born by the Holy Spirit through His earthly mother Mary, but was born of the tribe of Judah, and a loving stepfather, Joseph, who was also of the same lineage. His coming caused all of us to have the opportunity to be reunited again to our rich royal heritage. Jesus Christ did what no other deliverer had done for the people. He did not just die for them, but he became sin for them. The only way he could take on the whole world was through this reference: "For God was in Christ, reconciling the world to himself!" (2 Cor. 5:19) Many people have not yet acknowledged this wonderful divine connection yet; however, one day it will happen.

When you know who you are and from whence you've come, you have greater potential to lay claim to your life and future. You have much to live for and much to accomplish. Many people are just sitting back, waiting for someone else to do something for them. The pathway to your future is when you rise up and do what's inside of you to do. Accomplish your dream. Fulfill your divine purpose. Instead of waiting, take hold of what is yours. The dreams and visions in your head are not just wild imaginations, but literal pieces of your rich heritage and future undertakings. Your desires for the finer things in life are part of who you are. You are of royalty. You have ownership to all the rights and privileges of the kingdom. All you have to do is find out what they are and how to access each of them.

Chapter 7

Tru Faces Corruption and Violence

One day the evil genius, Triston, found a way to influence Tru's dreams. He wanted her dreams to become corrupt, so he could claim greatness for himself. Tru was really revered by everyone in her humble, noble city. The people knew she cared deeply for them because her dreams always, always came true for them. One day as she was listening intently to Amari, a well-known designer and toaster, the evil genius, Triston, was able to eavesdrop on their conversation and hear everything Amari told to Tru. After Tru left Amari to head home, Triston followed her and began to yell at her and say ugly things. He accused her of trying to help herself become great by doing things for others. He told her she was an evil witch because she read peoples' minds and cast spells on people. He told her that she would be cursed for her acts.

That night, Tru returned home and did not dream her usual good dreams. Instead, she actually dreamed a horrible dream about Amari's designer business closing down and all of his toast burning. The next day, Amari's bank found a miscalculation in his business account and accused him of fraud and closed his business down. He was so upset he burned all the toast and therefore, no one wanted any of his burnt toast. Needless to say, his toasting business went sour because he could no longer concentrate. He just kept burning all the toast. Tru began to question who she really was.

Tru felt horrible and responsible. She blamed herself for all the evil that was happening to people, and wondered why she was ever given such a terrible, unprofitable gift. Tru forgot about all the good that she had done for others. The evil genius, Triston, got what he wished. Slowly, people forgot all the good Tru had done and began to consult with Triston and he would listen and give them just enough to help them get by. The people learned to live on "just enough," but not without compromise, strife, and bitterness. Violence broke out in the noble city. Instead of people being noble, they became corrupt—liars, swindlers, gang bangers, drug dealers, bank robbers and selfish hardballs.

Tru had bad dreams continuously, and more bad things happened to the people. Tru believed she was to blame because of her bad dreams. Being the noble person that she was in her heart, Tru decided one day to travel to the Great City to see the Great King. No one seemed to notice her anymore, and the evil genius, Triston, forgot about her. She packed a small bag with her favorite teapot and slipped out of the city unnoticed. She walked and walked until she came upon a beautiful lily in the valley. The lily calmed her restless soul as she sat down to rest. As she rested, she picked some wild chamomile and made some tea. For some reason, the lily and tea reminded her of something or someplace she had been before. Her mind settled down and she continued on her journey.

Life Application #7

What has God Done for you?

 If people of today would just stop and rest their minds and think about what the Great God has done for mankind, they would realize He is not the kind that would withhold good things from them. The trickery would immediately stop, and life would begin—destiny would be fulfilled. Tru was deceived and tricked out of her true identity, yet inside she remained true to herself until she was able to find her way back to her true life. Every person can find his or her true identity, by looking within himself or herself and confessing the truth.

 Before you were here in the flesh, you were already in God's plan. The Great God said while man was fallen away in a very depraved condition, He established redemption and called it "His Personal Favor." We have the personal favor of the Great King. He also called it Grace and Kindness. Instead of condemning us for the wrong we have done, He made a sacrifice on our behalf and gave us another chance to live eternally outside of this fallen depraved condition. The Great King actually sent the Son of His Love as a substitute for all of us and called us back to Himself to live in royalty as priests and kings. (Eph. 2:5-8; John 3:16-17)

Again, no matter what wrong or evil you've done, He has already forgiven it. The Great King's personal favor has provided so much kindness to you until everything is available to you, such as your dreams—they can come true, your destiny is programmed for good, and your future is bright!

Chapter 8

Tru Recognizes Her True Identity, Part 1

Although Tru was on her way to see the Great King, she had no idea of how to get to the Great City. She walked and walked and was so tired until she started hearing voices. The voice was on the inside of her, encouraging her. She stopped at the edge of a beautiful garden of fruit and berries. Even this sight looked very familiar to her. Tru ate fruit and berries and fell fast asleep. As she slept, she dreamed of a beautiful palace with flowers and fruit all around. She saw children playing, singing and dancing. In the midst of the palace, she saw herself laughing, jumping, and leaping for joy. She was the happiest of all. Suddenly, she was awakened by a loud noise, but a sound she had heard before. It was the sound of a trumpet, and the entrance of the Great King. This time Tru was not having a dream or vision. The King's chamberlains (12 tall dark and handsome young men) dressed in royal attire with white, shining, glistening teeth and huge smiles surrounded Tru. They immediately lifted her onto a beautiful bed of gold, silk, and flowery coverings with a beautiful heavenly fragrance. Tru rose up to find she was being carried before the throne where the Great King was seated. The King had a great, big smile. The people in the Great City began to rejoice with praise, honor and glory, for the princess had come home. Tru was so noble because she was from the royal family of the Great King!

Tru was an American Princess all along. Her training had come from being a child of the King. She was born a princess. An American Princess is characterized by her qualities. Tru definitely shared the qualities of a princess. A princess of any nation, culture or family can be characterized by these qualities. A princess is a noble young lady who carries herself with poise and dignity. She listens attentively. And when she speaks, she carefully chooses her words. She exercises control over her emotions and makes choices based on what's right rather than on how she feels. Though she isn't perfect, she possesses a strong sense of duty that comes with knowing she's a princess. A princess thinks of others. She is trusting and faithful. Another princess virtue is humility. She doesn't demand or expect special treatment from others and chooses to refrain from bragging or boasting. Instead, she focuses on others and their needs. She doesn't have to be in the spotlight because she already knows she's a princess. A princess is extraordinarily beneficent. She is gentle, generous, compassionate, patient, good-natured and forgiving. A princess doesn't compete with her prince. She does just the opposite, she builds him up. It's her admiration and respect that inspire the prince and compel him to greatness. A princess is a princess regardless of her attire or her circumstances (urbandictionary.com). Her training had come from being a child of the King. The seed of righteousness was actually always there; she just lost her way and was deceived of her true identity.

Tru found out that the evil genius, Triston, had stolen her away years ago and held her in captivity in the little town of Tyrina, where people were not allowed to travel outside of their communities, and the children were not given very many books to read, and where the people were given jobs or businesses that would only profit them a little. Triston, the evil genius, wanted to keep them humble and he treated everyone as if he or she were less than he. Triston had a superior attitude and wanted people to know he was better than everyone else. Tru was supposed to be the answer to his dilemma. However, Tru remained noble because she was the daughter of a noble king. Although she was not aware of her true identity, she remained true to who she was on the inside. The evil genius, Triston, tried to influence her dreams, but little did he know that they were never her dreams that caused people's lives to be blessed; but rather it was her noble ways, her honest heart, and the secret of her true identity as princess.

Life Application #8

Power of Knowledge

There lies in each of us the secret of success and the key to true greatness. The evil genius wants to keep you deceived and held in captivity by the influences of this world. The true identity of any man or woman is hidden in the Great God who holds the key. Knowledge of the Great God unlocks the door. Some people get lost along the way and have to find their way back. Some people get tricked and walk around in deception living another life, when they could have been living the best life now! Success is the accomplishment of an aim or purpose, but true greatness comes from within. Greatness is the result of the application of the knowledge you acquire. Knowledge is power! Many people are destroyed for a lack of knowledge or because they reject the knowledge presented to them.

Knowledge can be defined as the facts, information, and skills acquired by a person through experience or education. It is also the theoretical understanding of a subject or the awareness or familiarity gained by experience of a fact or situation. If the creator of knowledge has all knowledge, then it is clear that more knowledge of the creator equals more facts, information, and skills that a person can acquire.

Chapter 9

Tru Recognizes Her True Identity, Part 2

Tru's purpose and destiny was inside of her all along, yet she lost her way and was deceived by evil. Her road to greatness came after much deception, rejection, hurt, and shame. Her noble heart and character are attributes that saved her life because at the end of the day, she looked within herself and dared to believe that she could find the Great City and experience true greatness. She decided to test and try her own dream about a land where there was a Great God and King where the desires of her heart could be met. She dreamt of a land where she could be blessed beyond measure, and she took a chance to find it.

Tru discovered her true identity. She was most definitely the daughter of the Great King of Lambert, the Great Country. The Great King served the Great God of Lambert, who would give anyone the desires of his or her heart. Though Tru was noble, the real meaning of her nobility was hidden in not only her true identity as princess of the Great Country, but also in the fact that she was also the Spear Maiden, which means that she has the strength of a spear and was able to see things that others could not see. She could see the visions in her head at night. Once a person shared his or her heart with Tru, she would be able to see the answer. She really did have the gifts of the Spirit to operate through her and she could not explain it. Tru's practices never changed; each night she would go home and kneel down before the Great God of Lambert and say, "Now, my God the King, reveal to me what your servant needs to know and grant your blessings unto those who are in need." As she would sleep upon her bed, the Great God of Lambert would speak to the Great King, who would hear and answer her prayers.

Tru, the Spear Maiden, had been hoping that one day she would dream for herself. She thought dreaming for her purposes was forbidden. This is what the evil genius used to trick her into captivity. Otherwise, she was so strong that nothing could defeat her. The Great King of Lambert was so noble that he could not set her free until she desired it for herself, even though she was his own daughter, the princess of the Great City of Lambert and served the Great God of Lambert. All people must realize their true identity and their own hidden gifts and talents. People of the Great Country have all been given the Gift of Sufficiency within themselves, but they must recognize it every day and utilize it in order to achieve great success in the land. The Great God of Lambert is the God who is more than enough. All of His people should live a life representing who He is. Anything less is not of the Great God!!!! Anyone who allows the people to only have just enough or not enough is someone who wants to control others and keep them captive. Succeeding and having more than enough is the way of the Great God of Lambert. Tru once knew her true identity but was deceived. In her heart she was still true to herself. In the town of Tyrina, she was practicing everything she knew that the Great God of Lambert willed for her life and others. However, evil was lurking everywhere because the people did not know about the Great God and the Great King. All could have had their deepest desires and their needs met daily, if they had only known about the Great King who desired to do so. Tru thought all of her visions were only crazy dreams, when actually she was having revelations of her kingdom.

Life Application #9

The Gift of Sufficiency

    You were born with gifts and talents. These gifts and talents cannot be removed or recalled by the one who places them in you, but they can be misused or used for less than royal means. When you use these God-given gifts and talents for true and genuine prosperity of the kingdom, you are proving that the Great King is a covenant-keeping, promise-keeping king. He wants us to know this about Him so that we can place more and more trust in His goodness and fairness as our Great King.

    The only way a person does not prosper and live in the blessings of his or her royal heritage is if he or she is actually deceived to think that the inheritance does not belong to him or her. This is what happened to Tru. She knew in her heart that she had a gift to offer and used it to influence others, but did not quite know how to use it for herself. People sometimes have really great gifts (and often more than one or two), but use them in the wrong way: from the Drug Dealer in your neighborhood (who makes money selling drugs to teens and adults), to the embezzler at a Fortune 500 company (who uses investors'

*funds for personal bonuses and salaries), to those who
sing, dance, and act (not for the glory of God, but rather at
the expense of degrading their own lives and the lives of
others). Just as each of these individuals can use their gifts
and talents for personal gain in the wrong way, they can
also use these same faculties in the right way for personal
gain and God's Glory. Identifying your innate gifts and
talents is very important. Your gifts and talents will cause
you to prosper and have wealth. Dr. Myles Munroe said it
best: "What you were designed to be known for is your gift.
God has put a gift or talent in every person that the world
will make room for—It is this gift that will enable you to
fulfill your vision. It will make a way for you in life. It is in
exercising this gift that you will find real fulfillment,
purpose, and contentment in your work."*

*The Great King always provides for his children,
especially those who honor the king and take part in their
inheritance. He is the King of everything and has made
provision for everything. He is called The Provider. Rick
Warren lets us know that gifts and talents can be used
improperly or to our advantage. He said, "You think your
talents are simply for you to make a lot of money, retire,
and die, you've missed the point of your life. God gave you*

talents to benefit others, not yourself. And God gave other people talents that benefit you." The Great King's heart's desire is for his children to walk as members of the royal family and reign as kings and priests of our domain.

Chapter 10

Tru's Return Home

After Tru returned to the Great City of Lambert, she began to take pleasure in her home and family. As a result, the great country began to prosper even the more. The Great King was able to help the people of Tyrina to be noble and true to themselves so that He could provide them with all that they could ask for or think of beyond their highest hopes and dreams. The Great City began to become greater and greater because Tru was back. The Noble city of Tyrina was set free from the evil genius, Triston, as Tru began to believe and express the desires of her heart. Her heart's desires and dreams came true because she remained noble in the toughest and darkest times of her life.

Life Application #10

Overcoming Dark and Tough Times

If you are facing captivity in some way right now or if you are going through dark and tough times in your life, all you have to do is look within and be true to yourself. You are fearfully and wonderfully made. In other words, you are God's handiwork. You are blessed and highly favored. You no longer have to believe the lies of the evil spirit of deception. Remember, there is an evil genius that is nothing short of brilliant at deceiving people. However, if you follow your heart and your dreams, you will find solace and rest for your soul. The troubles of this old world are not the essence of this life. The greatness of our God makes us great! He awaits the opportunity to share His greatness with us. God's greatness in us only starts when we look inside and identify with the person He has made each of us to be as we share our gifts and talents with our world each day.

Chapter 11

Back in the Noble City of Tyrina

Back in the noble city of Tyrina, Amari's business was returned to him because the banker dreamed of his own mistake and, because he was noble, returned everything (and more) to Amari. Tru was old enough now to understand her reign as princess. When her father, the Great King, knew that she was ready, he would relinquish the entire rulership of the Great Country to her.

Even the evil genius, Triston, was released from captivity. Tru dreamed that Triston was tricked into thinking that, in order to have success, he had to control others and force them to serve him. He wanted people to believe that he was the one they should look to for their well being, and he wanted them to believe that they were less than he. In Triston's evil and twisted mind, he knew if people did not know their true identities, then he had the main tool to capture them and force them to a life of "just enough or not enough." This type of behavior always causes one nation to bow down to another. He knew he would have control of their minds, welfare, and ultimately their lives. The problem is that most people do not believe in a God who is "more than enough." They do not believe that He will supply "ALL your needs according to His riches in Glory" by the Great King of all kings (Phil. 4:19 KJV).

Tru released Triston from his torment. She had a magnificent revelation. Triston was actually the Prince of Lonne', the global country of the land next door. Triston was really Lionheart, meaning "Strong as a Lion." Tru, "the Spear Maiden," and Lionheart, "Strong as a Lion," lived happily ever after, reigning as the Queen and King of both countries. Because of their noble hearts, they were always regarded as the Prophetess and Priest of the times. They taught the people daily in the great temple. Millions began to return to the great temple regularly for worship. The noble city of Tyrina was really the "City of Worship," but had been led into the captivity of the evil one. People rarely attended the great temple because there were so many things going on to keep them too busy to go inside.

Inside the great temple, the prophetesses and the prophets were teaching the truth about the Great God of Lambert so that each person would know their true identity. Tru and Lionheart were able to help them discover the real key to greatness, as they had discovered it.

Life Application #11

Worship, a Key Ingredient

    Personal worship is a key ingredient to knowing who you are in the kingdom of the Great King. Since the people of Tyrina failed to attend worship, it affected their way of life. True worship is not a little thing; but many times in life, the little things that we overlook may be the very things that make the difference—had we taken heed. The key to true greatness was in Tyrina right in the midst of the people all along, though they failed to take time to go into the temple for worship. You may be going along in life right now and have a successful job or business, or school may be going great and grades are up, and life is good; but what if you are neglecting the one thing that will put you over in life in every area? You may feel there is no need for it. The area of need may not have even come up yet; however, you should want to be prepared when it does come.

    What could possibly be inside the great temple that could put someone over in life?

First of all, "to worship" means to:

- *Give God your best*

- *Offer back to Him what He gives to you (your utmost for His highest)*

- *Express reverence and adoration to*

- *Honor with extravagant love and extreme submission*

[Source: Webster's Dictionary, 1828]

Second, true worship is defined by the priority we place on who the Great King is in our lives and where He is on our list of priorities. True worship is a matter of the heart expressed through a lifestyle of holiness.

Third, it is highly appropriate to thank the Great King for all He is doing, has done, and is going to do; but it is an all-time high to worship Him for who He is to us! True worship allows the Great King to reveal Himself to us and manifest Himself to us. There will be things that happen to you in your life for which you will have no answer, no explanation, and no other evidence. Yet, you will know that it is He on display in your life. The manifestation of His power to you will be displayed and you will identify His mighty acts!

Something happens in the great temple that is beyond natural explanations. John said it this way: "Beloved, now are we the sons of God" (1 John 3:2 KJV). When we come into the presence of a Mighty King as a son or daughter, we are privileged to have whatever the king has and we are granted unconditional love and blessings. We are the sons and daughters of a royal heritage. The Great King will manufacture what his children are in need of. He gives His children the best, as would any loving father. Because of the power that's working in us, He will do much more than whatever we ask him to do or whatever we are thinking He will do (Eph. 3:20).

Chapter 12

Tru Used Her Gifts and Talents for the Prosperity of the People

Princess and Prophetess Tru used her gift and noble heart daily as she approached the Great God of Lambert of the Great Country for the desires of her heart. He continued to show her things through her dreams and visions. All her dreams continued to come true, once again. Tru, the true Spear Maiden, would speak words of encouragement and comfort to the hearts of people. She would teach them how to look within and identify the origin of true peace and joy. She taught them how to follow the goodness in their hearts and not all the negative influences from without. She said, "If you keep your hearts right and never agree with the evil influences, the Great God of Lambert will bring to pass all that you can ask or think, even your highest hopes and dreams." The people found out that it was not just Tru who was special, or that only her dreams came true, but their dreams, too.

Priest-Prophet Lionheart was strong as a lion and used his gift of influence and noble heart to speak simple words of wisdom. He would stand in strength and power, and all the people would bow their knees and say the Great God of Lambert lives in Priest Lionheart. Because Lionheart was no longer the evil genius, he would tell the people not to bow to him, but rather to the Great God of Lambert. He no longer wanted to have rulership over the people's hearts and lives. He wanted them to worship the Great God of Lambert and live noble lives on their own. He also wanted them to have more than enough to live healthy and wealthy lives. He had discovered that sickness, disease, poverty, violence and evil in the land are all because of someone exerting the evil power of "lack" and "just enough" over another. After he was released from the evil power of "lack" and "just enough," he now had the gift of giving in his life; and everyone in his Great Country had more than enough on which to live, and was generous to others. These were very contagious noble acts that were spreading everywhere, even in the lands down under.

Tru and Lionheart not only lived happily ever after

as the Noble Queen and King, but also as the Prophetess and Priest who operated in strength and power, saving the

world from destruction and famine through their wisdom, might and noble hearts.

Life Application #12

Use Your Gifts and Talents for the Prosperity of Others so That You Can Prosper, too

Once you realize who you are and what you are capable of doing, there are no limits to your success. Each Application of Life Lesson needs to be applied in your life to ensure your future. Don't miss out and feel sorry for yourself for not achieving your life's purpose when you can get inspired now and go forth and achieve greatness. Whatever is inside of you right now is there for your prosperity and the good of others. Forget about all the past issues and hurts. All of us have been abused, misused and hurt in some way in life. Some of us were just a little more resilient than others and bounced back on track, but the Great King had to nudge others a little more to get their attention. The evil genius has been let loose from his assignment against you. You are not deceived any longer. You know who you are—a son or daughter of the Great King. You are of the royal family of the Great King! You are an heir and a joint-heir with all the Blessed Kingdom People! The Great King has sponsored you, Himself. His personal favor is upon you! You can make a public profession, "I am a child of the King."

The secret of true freedom lies in having the knowledge that one can have the desires of his or her heart met or fulfilled. Somewhere deep inside of Tru, she had a seed of knowing that there was a Great Country somewhere that was better. This knowledge was deeper than natural knowledge or sense knowledge. It was revealed in that place within that causes one to know something without being told something first. The evil genius, who is also the great deceiver, deceives people (including the American girl) into not desiring anything for themselves, just to keep them in captivity. This deception is very strong and hidden because it is mixed with an element of truth which makes it difficult to discern at times. It will hinder growth of a confident and strong person who normally manages well in all three areas of life (spirit, soul, and body). The American girl's journey was not unlike many of ours. She was in search of her true identity and the Great Country. She did a lot of good along the way, but encountered hard times. She chose some of the unwise decisions, but the others were due to deception. Like many of us, we chose some of the things in our past, but some were due to the deception in our minds. As Tru uses the gift of dreams to help her fellow citizens, she fails to use it for herself. (This is deception.) Some people use their gifts for evil and to take from others. (This is also deception.) Some people use their gifts and talents to work for the good of others. (This is the plan of God.) Tru finds her way in life and helps to uncover her true identity, and she helps the evil genius to uncover his, also. The power and anointing upon her life first brings her to the palace of the King, and then it brings a shining light on the operation of a horrible spirit of deception and trickery operating through Triston. She releases him from captivity.

Chapter 13

The Life of An American Princess or Prince, Whether African, Asian, Hispanic, Native American, or Dutch

The story reveals why you dream and your dreams come true, so that each of you reading this book will understand how to tap into your dreams to fulfill your purpose in life. By examining your dreams, you, too, will discover your true identity. You will discover the reason you are here on this earth at this season of life. You have something that this world needs. It's worth a lot to a lot of people. Intentionally discover your gift and purposely use it for the glory of the King. You are here for purpose and because you are connected to the Great King of kings, "He will make you perfect in every good thing to do His will, working in you that which is well pleasing in His sight (Hebrews 13:21 ASV)." This is so amazing, and He can do this in all of us in His Kingdom at the same time. The

Great King gives each of us THE gift, but there is an evil genius waiting to snatch it away.

Your most prominent gift may not be the gift of dreams (as Tru possessed), but whatever your gift is—He will make it perfect in you for every good thing!

About The Author

Warren and Linda Trimble Ministries

Linda was born in Oak Ridge, LA, but reared in Monroe, LA. She was Born-again and filled with the Spirit at a very early age. Linda is a graduate of Northeast Louisiana University with a Master's of Education degree and Counseling Certification. Linda is a woman is wisdom and truly has the virtues of a Proverbs 31 woman. Linda serves with her husband, Warren, on the Pastoral staff of LCC. She is also one of the leading women mentors and speakers in this area today. They both are graduates of Liberty School of Ministry and Bible Institute. Linda is the founder of Celebrating Women--an outreach to women in the community. This outreach celebrates women for their accomplishments and service to their communities, churches, and civic organizations. She is also the Conference Host and Founder of the United Fellowship of Women, a worldwide network of women uniting together in love from all walks of life.

Warren and Linda are called to do the work of the ministry. They work in the ministry together and focus on areas of ministry that will bless the entire family. They have a dynamic outreach to married couples, youth, church family, and are active community members. Because of their own personal testimonies, love for others in their heart, and the anointing upon their lives, they do not just preach and teach the Gospel of Jesus Christ without compromise, but also live as Kingdom Ambassadors. As they share the Word of God with humor, they will also help you to understand the practical application of the Word in your personal life. Their 30-plus years experience in ministry, education and life will minister to your entire family—while the Word changes you forever.

Their mission is to change the lives of people through teaching and practical applications of the fundamentals of the Word. As men, women and children receive the Word of God, the truth will make them free. Free from the poverty, sickness and oppression of the devil. Our aim is to teach people to live by faith and to let them know that they can live holy- separated lives every day.

As the message is demonstrated around the world, lives are changed. Warren and Linda serve people without regard to race, color, ethnic origin, creed, or religious affiliation. As people hear and apply the Word, they develop to their fullest potential and fulfill their God-ordained destinies.

Contact Information for speaking engagement, book information, or to visit a life changing ministry:
Warren & Linda Trimble Ministries
P O Box 7481
Monroe, LA 71211
318-327-5974
web: libertysoutheast.com
email: lindalawsontrimble@gmail.com

Notes

1. deceived - (Merriam-Webster.com) Citation [Def. 4]. (n.d.). In Merriam Webster Online, Retrieved May, 27, 2014, from http://www.merriam-webster.com/dictionary/citation.

2. Ralph Waldo Emerson (quotationspage.com) Moncur. M. (2015, January 9). The Quotation Page. Retrieved from www.quotationspage.com

3. Walt Disney (pslinstitute.com) Engelbreit, M. (2015, January 9). Personal Success and Leadership Institute. Retrieved from www.pslinstitute.com.

4. Anglican Bishop (necessity4failure.com) Elkhart. (2012, Dec. 5). Joy in a Roman Jail. Retrieved from www.neccessity4failure.com

5. Jakes (huffingtonpost.com) Huffington, Arianna. (2014, May 7). Oprah's Life Class. Retrieved from www.huffingtonpost.com.

6. Jeremiah 29:11 (New International Version)

7. Success is the favorable . . . (dictionary.reference.com) Citation [Def. 1]. (n.d.). Dictionary.com Online, Retrieved Jan 9, 2014, from http://dictionary.reference.com/browse/success?s=t

8. Norman Vincent (quotationspage.com) Moncur. M. (2015, January 9). The Quotation Page. Retrieved from www.quotationspage.com

9. Jerry Bruckner (get successquotes.com) Bruckner. J. (2015, January 9). Get SuccessQuotes.com. Retrieved from www.getsuccessquotes.com

10. Eleanor Roosevelt (brainyquote.com) Proverbia. (2015, Jan. 9). Proverbs. Retrieved from http://en.proverbia.net/proverbs.asp

11. 17.6 million people, or one in every 12 adults, suffer . . . (ncadd.org) (January 9, 2015). Learn About Alcohol: FAQ's Facts. Retrieved from http://ncadd.org/learn-about-alcohol/faqsfacts

13. Gang joining & risk factors (nationalgangcenter.gov) (2015, Jan. 9) National Gang Center. Retrieved from https://www.nationalgangcenter.gov/

14. Dr. Myles Munroe - What you were designed to be known for is your gift . . .Triplett, G. (2015, January 22). Your Gift Will Make Room For You! [Gillis Triplett Ministries]. Retrieved from http://www.gillistriplett.com/manhood/articles/yourgift.html

15. Rick Warren - quote - " You think your talents are simply for you to make a lot of money . . .Warren, R. (2014, May 21). Make The Most of Your Talents [Daily Hope]. Retrieved from http://rickwarren.org/devotional/english/make-the-most-of-your-talents

STRONG
PUBLISHING
House

bringing the strength of your words to reality

If you would like to order more copies of this book or other publications, please contact Strong Publishing House via email at strongpublishinghouse@gmail.com
or
Visit our website at
www.strongpublishinghouse.com

www.ingramcontent.com/pod-product-compliance
Lightning Source LLC
Chambersburg PA
CBHW062018040426
42447CB00010B/2054